*The Prophetic Flow of Healing and Deliverance*

# The Prophetic Flow of Healing and Deliverance

POEMS BY

## FLORINE G. FREEMAN

XULON ELITE

Xulon Press Elite
2301 Lucien Way #415
Maitland, FL 32751
407.339.4217
www.xulonpress.com

© 2023 by Florine G. Freeman

Contribution by:Carol Myrthil-Dickerson

All rights reserved solely by the author. The author guarantees all contents are original and do not infringe upon the legal rights of any other person or work. No part of this book may be reproduced in any form without the permission of the author. The views expressed in this book are not necessarily those of the publisher.

Due to the changing nature of the Internet, if there are any web addresses, links, or URLs included in this manuscript, these may have been altered and may no longer be accessible. The views and opinions shared in this book belong solely to the author and do not necessarily reflect those of the publisher. The publisher, therefore, disclaims responsibility for the views or opinions expressed within the work.

Unless otherwise indicated, Scripture quotations taken from the King James Version (KJV)–*public domain.*

Paperback ISBN-13: 978-1-66287-012-5
Ebook ISBN-13: 978-1-66287-013-2

# Acknowledgements

I give all the glory to God my Creator and Heavenly Father, and my Lord and Savior, Jesus Christ. I thank God for entrusting me with His gifts and I'm grateful to be His daughter; serving Him is my main priority. I honor and love my parents who've passed on; they embedded the Word of God and the principles of life in me. My family is phenomenal, and I'm sincerely thankful for their support. I appreciate all Pastors that imparted the power of faith into my life.

# Dedication

**I'd like to dedicate this book to my beloved parents, John H. Freeman and Henrietta Freeman who have transitioned to glory.**

# Table of Contents

Acknowledgements. . . . . . . . . . . . . . . . . . . . . . . . . . . . . . . . . v
Dedication. . . . . . . . . . . . . . . . . . . . . . . . . . . . . . . . . . . . . . . vii
Introduction . . . . . . . . . . . . . . . . . . . . . . . . . . . . . . . . . . . . . xi

POWER OF THE SPOKEN WORD . . . . . . . . . . . 1
MY FAITH TESTIMONY . . . . . . . . . . . . . . . . . . . . 3
Prayer of Faith:. . . . . . . . . . . . . . . . . . . . . . . . . . . . . . . . . . .6
I LIVE . . . . . . . . . . . . . . . . . . . . . . . . . . . . . . . . . . . . . 7
ROYALTY. . . . . . . . . . . . . . . . . . . . . . . . . . . . . . . . . 9
FAITH. . . . . . . . . . . . . . . . . . . . . . . . . . . . . . . . . . . 11
DEPRESSION. . . . . . . . . . . . . . . . . . . . . . . . . . . . 13
TRADITION AND RELIGION . . . . . . . . . . . . . . 16
WHAT TIME IS IT? . . . . . . . . . . . . . . . . . . . . . . . . 19
LOVE . . . . . . . . . . . . . . . . . . . . . . . . . . . . . . . . . . . 21
THE PLOT. . . . . . . . . . . . . . . . . . . . . . . . . . . . . . . 24
RESURRECTED . . . . . . . . . . . . . . . . . . . . . . . . . . 26
THE KINGDOM . . . . . . . . . . . . . . . . . . . . . . . . . . 29
ANGELIC ASSISTANCE . . . . . . . . . . . . . . . . . . . 32
HALLELUJAH, A PSALM OF PRAISE. . . . . . . . 35

Flo's Quotes. . . . . . . . . . . . . . . . . . . . . . . . . . . . . . . . . . . . . . . 38

Scripture References . . . . . . . . . . . . . . . . . . . . . . . . . . . . . . 43

References . . . . . . . . . . . . . . . . . . . . . . . . . . . . . . . . . . . . . . . .53

Bio . . . . . . . . . . . . . . . . . . . . . . . . . . . . . . . . . . . . . . . . . . . . . .55

# Introduction

In 2006, my passion for poetry was inspired. For many years, I desired to express my thoughts in writing, but I struggled with confidence. My past experiences enlightened me to pursue this art. I went to several spoken word shows, where poets articulated their gift. This was my first introduction to poetry and the cultivation process began. I started writing and became comfortable with my work. As I performed at shows, my confidence level grew immensely. One should never despise small beginnings. God will use people to bring out of you, what He has already placed in you.

# POWER OF THE SPOKEN WORD

*I* am an artist of poetry. Poetry is the art of the spoken word through expressions of one's intellect, experience, wisdom, knowledge, understanding, dreams and visions. *For to one is given by the Spirit the word of wisdom; to another the word of knowledge by the same Spirit; I Cor. 12:8.* Fundamentally it's the foundation of one of God's profound creations. I embrace poetry as a spiritual gift that ignites a fire derived from the depths of my existence. *Every good gift and every perfect gift is from above, and cometh down from the Father of lights, with whom is no variableness, neither shadow of turning. James 1:17.* God has endowed me with many gifts. The exploration of poetry gives me liberation. Words that we speak carry power for activation. *Death and life are in the power of the tongue: and they that love it shall eat the fruit thereof. Proverbs 18:21.* We must be careful of the seeds we sow with words. Positive words produce positive results and negative words produce negative results. *"Be not rash with thy mouth, and let not thine heart utter anything before God" Eccl. 5:2.* It's imperative to speak life, success, good health, fruitfulness and things that will ultimately prosper you. God desires for you and I to speak positively and with his authority. Words can create change in the atmosphere. God created His creations from His words and since we are created in His image and likeness, we can do the same, in Jesus Name! *So God created man in his own image, in the image of God created he him; male and female created he them. Gen. 1:27.* God is righteous; therefore we should live and speak righteously. By adhering to the Word of God, you will produce righteous living in abundance. I pray that when you read these words of inspiration, you receive deliverance and multiple revelations. This impartation will give you strength and rejuvenation to speak positive declarations. This is your beginning of a new spoken word. God Bless You!

# MY FAITH TESTIMONY

*O*n May 1, 2004, The Holy Spirit instructed me to attend a "Spring Gospel Concert" on the Southside of Chicago. I didn't have any money and my gas hand was on E. I asked my mother if I could borrow some money, but she didn't have it. The Lord spoke to my spirit and said, "You have Faith, Trust Me and GO." My mother told me not to go, but I said I have to obey God. In the natural it looked impossible, but I stepped into the supernatural realm and grabbed on to Faith believing that God would make a way. I obeyed and went. When I arrived, the ticket agent said that all tickets had been sold. I went to the restroom and prayed and told God, I obeyed you, so I need you to perform a MIRACLE. Suddenly, I hear two young ladies saying they had an extra ticket. I asked them if I could have the ticket, but they said it cost $15. I told them I didn't have any money and God told me to come to the concert by Faith and I obeyed Him. They were looking at me strange, but I didn't care because I was trusting God until the end. I spoke boldly and said, "If you bless me with this ticket, GOD IS GOING TO MOVE IN THIS CONCERT". They agreed and gave me a V.I.P. ticket.

I began to rejoice and thank God for my MIRACLE. We walked in while the choir was singing and sat down. One of the ladies dared me to start dancing in the aisle. I stepped in the aisle and began to dance before the Lord and praise God. I went to the altar and bowed worshipping God, because of my MIRACLE. I know people were looking at me crazy, but I blocked everyone out of my mind and glorified God because He didn't make me ashamed. I left out the church to go fix my clothing. That same young lady followed me and said that the concert host was calling me to the stage. I literally was shocked. However, I walked in the church, and everyone was smiling and applauding. The host called me to the stage and told me that he received a note that God told me to come to the concert by Faith and someone blessed me with a ticket. I agreed that it was true. He told me that God was going to bless me because of my Faith. I was in awe that my Father God stopped a concert for me. As I started to leave the stage, the host called me and gave me $20, then another came and gave me $20, then everyone started to come and throw money at my feet. I began to cry and glorify God. I fell down and people were throwing money on my body. The host had me to sit on the front row. The concert continued and then came to a pause. A group of pastors and ministers called me up and prayed for me. They said they had to seal the blessing on me and told me that the anointing of wealth was on my life. The host never asked my name, but he gave me the microphone to say, "Thank you". I was given an envelope and blessed with over $2000. After the concert people were still giving me money. God caused an overflow to manifest. The host assigned two young men to trail me home. One young man trailed me to the gas station, because my car was on E. He filled my tank up with gas. When I arrived home and told my mother, she was so happy that I obeyed God and not her. LOL! The Lord instructed me to first pay my tithes and give an offering, then financially bless my mother, brothers, sisters, friends and to put myself last. You should never forget to sow into those who sowed into you; The Lord had me to release an offering to the host, because he obeyed God. All increase comes from God, so when God blesses me, I sow back into the kingdom. Obedience will release supernatural provisions and blessings and Faith will unlock MIRACLES and cause God to perform on your behalf. Faith and boldness is a requirement for obedience. Your yes to God, will cause others to say yes to God!

# Prayer of Faith:

Father God, in the Name of Jesus your Word says in Rom. 10:17 that "Faith cometh by hearing and hearing by the Word of God"; so, I pray that every reader receives the revelation of Faith in their heart, so they can experience the supernatural power of God. Amen!

# I LIVE

I live to be free

I live to be who God made me to be

I live for security

I live to avoid obscurity

I live to help someone who's in pain

I live not in vain

I live to be an example for Christ

I live also to gain eternal life

I live to embrace intellect

I live to learn new dialects

I live for success and achievement

I live to gain strength through bereavement

I live to experience agape love

I live to receive blessings from heaven above

I live to explore and expand my territory

I live and exist because of God's glory

*But thou shalt remember the Lord thy God: for it is he that giveth thee power to get wealth, that he may establish his covenant which he sware unto thy fathers, as it is this day. Deuteronomy 8:18.*

# ROYALTY

You are a King and Queen, clothed by God in righteousness, as you adore and worship His majesty. Arraigned and fashioned in his glorious image: spiritually, mentally, physically, emotionally and financially, who is destined for a dynasty. Royalty is your name! In Joel 2:26, God proclaims....."*and my people shall never be ashamed*". You are the epitome of Royalty! So arise and take your rightful place and decree His authority, which represents the majority. He chose you as peculiarity, so you can rise through all of your disparity by declaring freedom and walk in your days of pleasure and prosperity. After knowing this, you should stop seeking popularity from the world and keep in mind that God chose you before the foundation of the world. You are fearfully and wonderfully made, hand-crafted by God like the color of jade. The worth that you possess is more precious than rubies, which Jesus already paid. The essence of your divine nature will never age, and it will never fade, because you: my father, mother, brother, sister, son, daughter and friend.....you are

ROYALTY!

*"I will praise thee; for I am fearfully and wonderfully made..." Psalms 139:14.*

# FAITH

*I* heard by reading God's Word that, *"...faith cometh by hearing, and hearing by the word of God." Rom. 10:17* This is the start of the heart of faith. *"Now faith is the substance of things hoped for, the evidence of things not seen" Heb.11:1.* It's a stream of radical belief that liberates you in a place of God's peace and relief. Faith is spiritually tangible, because it's supernatural. We need to speak things that are not, as though they already are. This is divinely spectacular; you and I represent God's caliber. Faith is accessed through the supernatural; it can't be conceived in the natural. In the beginning when God created the heavens and the earth, he spoke the words; *"...Let there be..." Gen. 1:3,* and then appeared the light, the universe and His other creations were dispersed. Faith is now! Faith is not later! I'm a faith-taker, not a faith-waiter! I'm a faith-talker and a faith-walker! I'm a faith-doer and a faith-mover! I'm a faith-receiver and a faith-believer! We are made in the image and likeness of God, so we possess His same attributes. Without faith you will be spiritually mute. This is not something you can refute, but you might try to dispute. I'm speaking the truth!

The Prophetic Flow of Healing and Deliverance ~ 11

*But without faith it is impossible to please him: for he that cometh to God must believe that he is, and that he is a rewarder of them that diligently seek him. Hebrews 11:6.*

# DEPRESSION

*D*epression is a downward cycle. I classify it as a psychological spiral. This temporal process causes the mind to perceive negative connotations subconsciously. Depression leads you to a feeling of loneliness and despondency. There are horrid thoughts of contemplation of suicide, which penetrate throughout your intellect a few times. Mentally you try to navigate around what appears to be a hopeless fate. While others taunt and debase you, the emotions inside continue to grow and chase you. I prayed to God, will you please erase this pain, because I refuse to go insane. Depression is a downward cycle. I classify it as a psychological spiral. You find yourself seeking the opinion of a counselor or psychiatrist. One of their solutions are to prescribe an anti-depressant to suppress those feelings of fear, anxiety, stress and depression. I experienced many days of countless sessions and I consider my doctor as a blessing. However, the medicine didn't heal me. Depression will make you feel like you're deranged and have you acting a bit strange, but I declare that you're not insane. The things that occurred in your past, you must let them go, forgive yourself and others who you tend to blame. Depression is a downward cycle. I classify it as a psychological spiral. There is deliverance in Jesus, you should read the Bible. Jesus healed, delivered and set me free from the power of darkness that no longer captivates me. I'm a walking miracle and I give glory to God who is all superior. Jesus is healing you now from all bondage, condemnation, fear, guilt and shame in Jesus Name. There is power in His name. *Therefore if any man be in Christ, he is a new creature; old things are passed away; behold, all things are become new. 2 Cor. 5:17. You* will never be another victim of depression. As long as Jesus lives in your heart, he'll give you his love, joy, peace, power, thoughts, direction and protection.

*For God hath not given us the spirit of fear; but of power, and of love, and of a sound mind.* 2 Timothy 1:7.

# TRADITION AND RELIGION

*T*radition and religion make the Word of God of none effect; when you embrace these works of the flesh: witchcraft, emulations, idolatry and heresies. Maybe we've become complacent, and I make no apologies for this bold statement. Some of us glory in the outward appearance and we should seek God for a new experience. God examines the heart of a man; we should allow Him to do surgery on us, so he can remove every hinderance. We shouldn't walk around condemning others that don't look like us if we claim to be one of God's children. Now, The Holy-Spirit is a teacher, he'll give us what to say, how to dress and will teach us fervently how to pray. *For by grace are ye saved through faith; and that not of yourselves: it is the gift of God. Not of works, lest any man should boast. Eph. 2:8-9.* Let's walk in the fear of God and get delivered from religious yokes. I'm speaking the truth and addressing religious folks. The love of Jesus and his anointing will destroy every yoke. Tradition and religion make the Word of God of none effect; when you embrace these works of the flesh:

- **Witchcraft** is "...communication with the devil..." (Webster, 1983, p. 1354). This is a form of control, manipulation and deception.

- **Emulations** are "...ambition or endeavor to equal or excel others..." (Webster 1983, p. 408). This means to be in competition.

- **Idolatry** is "the worship of a physical object as a god..." (Webster 1983, p. 598). It is described as reverencing something as a superior being.

- **Heresies** are "...an opinion or doctrine contrary to church dogma..." (Webster 1983, p. 566). In other words, an individual's perception that opposes Christian beliefs.

There are other works of the flesh, but in Gal. 5:20 these four seem to dominate the rest. *So then they that are in the flesh cannot please God. Rom. 8:8.* The word encourages us to operate in the fruit of the Spirit. *"But the fruit of the Spirit is love, joy, peace, longsuffering, gentleness, goodness, faith, Meekness, temperance" Gal. 5:22-23.* By walking in obedience to the Word of God, we receive deliverance.

*Making the word of God of none effect through your tradition, which ye have delivered: and many such like things do ye. Mark 7:13.*

~

*There is therefore now no condemnation to them which are in Christ Jesus, who walk not after the flesh, but after the Spirit. Romans 8:1.*

# WHAT TIME IS IT?

Now is the time to change your life
This world is full of envy and strife
You should make Jesus your choice
So that you may always embrace His voice
Sound the alarm on Mt. Zion
The Enemy has come to devour as a lion

*For God hath not given us the spirit of fear; but of power,
and of love, and of a sound mind. 2 Tim. 1:7.*

Gird up your loins and let's put Satan in a bind
God has given us authority and power over Satan
There's no need to be afraid, just become blatant
The Word of God encourages us to make haste
Therefore, we have no time to waste
Jesus is soon to rapture all His saints
Make sure you use your power and don't faint

*Behold, I give unto you power, to tread upon serpents and scorpions and over all the power of the enemy and nothing shall by any means hurt you. Luke 10:19.*

# LOVE

When I think of love, I think of you

It's the way you smile that make my feelings true

Yes, it is overdue because of the delay

Sometimes I felt like I was falling astray

Just as one day, I was hit with a blow, but I knew

That I could get through this minor bliss

Appearing as a mist, that will simply fade away

Your love was made to stay in a way that soothes my soul

It will never grow old, because as long as I'm with you

I can conquer anything, for example one Spring

When one who is known as the King of Kings

Broke out with a bling and Ladies, I'm talking about a spiritual ring

He asked me to sing Him a love song, as I worshipped Him at home

I sighed and blushed, because of this constant rush of my heart

Skipping a beat, that I can't defeat, because my heart can't lie

So, I couldn't try to fight the feeling, knowing that it was revealing

My passion for Him through my daily fashion and compassion

Of my undeniable, unavoidable, unstoppable love for Him

In order to experience this type of love, I recommend that you

Engulf yourself with God's love, which comes from above

This is pure agape love

*He that loveth not, knoweth not God; for God is love. 1 John 4:8.*

# THE PLOT

The Enemy will try to sabotage your name, by digging up archives from the past, which are no longer the same. There is no need to be ashamed, because you have embraced your new change. We all have sinned and made foolish mistakes. When you repent, God will erase all of the filth away. Don't allow rumors to throw you off course. Walk in your authority, "...*and the violent take it by force*" Matt. 11:12. Remember, God is the only infallible source. These things are set up as a distraction. People want to see a natural reaction. Do the opposite and take spiritual action. Cancel every negative word, that's contrary to the truth of God's Word. This will give you satisfaction. I'm just being transparent and practical. Vengeance is not yours; it belongs to God. He will vindicate you. Continue to love and pray for your enemies, they'll soon be your footstool. God will restore everything the Enemy has stolen from you. Read Joel 2:25, his Word is true. *For he shall give his angels charge over thee, to keep thee in all thy ways. Psalms 91:11.*

*For all have sinned, and come short of the Glory of God; Romans 3:23.*

# RESURRECTED

*A*s I began to evaluate my surroundings, I realized that this evidence was false appearing to be real,

this is not God's will for my life, so I've learned through this to be still and hear his voice, avoiding

all others....I must rejoice, because the Enemy thought this was my final demise, but God allowed me

another chance to arise, as I dance and glorify Him is the ultimate high............you see Satan only attack those who he's threatened by, since he know his time is drawing nigh........................WOW! I'm still here,

after fear tried to destroy and take my sanity, I thank God for the trinity, what a combination of God's triune creation.....................my family didn't have to put me away and throw away the key, because before the foundation of the world God chose and ordained me already FREE... ......I've been sealed in His righteousness.......isn't that a mystery!!!

God reminded me that I was created in His image and originated only from his lineage........I'll never again return to that place called Babylon, because I'm apart of the kingdom of God..............

The bible says that certain things only come by fasting and praying, I understand by this sacrifice

you can save your life.........from these demons, because God has made me a FREE-MAN, by sending His son, Jesus to die on the cross for every soul not to be lost.................. this was the priceless cost paid for humanity.................. .........Y'all I still got my sanity.....................Jesus washed away these calamities..............................yes I choose to be repetitious, because I was presented with something fictitious............................

through this experience, I'll always remember to..."*believe not every spirit, but try the spirits*

*whether they are of God*" 1 John 4:1.....many spirits are a facade........I declare that my final chapter is not in my vocabulary........................

life is taking off for me and it's the beginning of a new sanctuary...................living in the land flowing with milk and honey, collecting my wealth which includes my money... ...........I AM VICTORIOUS AND I GIVE GLORY TO GOD WHO IS ALL GLORIOUS! Seeing your-self resurrected and FREE is pure DESTINY, and this is my DECREE.....in Jesus Name, I AM FOREVER FREE!!!

*Beloved, believe not every spirit, but try the spirits whether they are of God: because many false prophets are gone out into the world. 1 John 4:1.*

# THE KINGDOM

*I*n this season God is raising up His sons and daughters in the earth to manifest His kingdom.

God has released a greater fire upon His church to flow in a new level of wisdom, understanding, revelation knowledge, authority, peace and freedom.

The Holy Spirit is giving us the answer and the solutions through meditation of the Word, dreams and visions. God has already given us access to our provisions.

The glory of the Lord shall be revealed in a soniferous way that naysayers won't be able to deny the demonstrations that shall take place.

We will not be moved or shaken by what we see in the natural, because God has given us spiritual vision and insight to flow in the realm of the supernatural.

Psalms 125:1 says, They that trust in the Lord shall be as mount Zion which cannot be removed, but abideth forever. Through the anointing, God is taking his church to another level, and he's given us authority to tread over every scorpion, demon and devil.

The anointing of God is upon us to destroy yokes and minister deliverance to the lost and religious folks.

The wisdom in us will attract wealth and ignite the transfer of more wealth. We shall build and advance the kingdom of God through preaching the gospel, taking care of the widows and orphans, providing for the less fortunate, establishing businesses and building schools.

Faith is the driving force for the kingdom of heaven suffers violence and the violent take it by force. We the church are taking territory by walking in our God-given kingdom authority. For it is God in us that's doing the work and we shall manifest His glory.

God has given us a kingdom mandate in the earth to dominate, be fruitful and plant the heavens. There's a wealth portal open and in the garden of Eden we shall flourish.

*They that trust in the Lord shall be as mount Zion which cannot be removed, but abideth for ever. – Psalms 125:1*

# ANGELIC ASSISTANCE

*G*od has created His children a little lower than the angels and he's given us power to access our Angels.

Our Angels represent supernatural assistance and will help fight off demonic resistance; by preserving us as we submit to God in service. The Angels of the Lord encamps around those who fear God for this is their charge and purpose.

They'll respond to us by the Word of activation, but it'll only work by the Word of faith, meditation and declaration.

God has given us the authority to give our Angels assignments and they shall hearken to the command of the Word of God with no confinement.

Angels will deliver thoughts, ideas, messages, instructions and directions. They were designed to give us divine protection. This is a blessing from Heaven.

Angels can also appear in a dream or an open vision; this is apart of our kingdom inheritance provision.

We need our Angels and the Bible tells us they may even come in the form of a stranger; and yes they'll protect us from all hurt, harm and danger.

The Angels were created by God to worship God and cover the children of God.

*The angel of the Lord encampeth round about them that fear him, and delivereth them.*
*Psalms 34:7*

# HALLELUJAH, A PSALM OF PRAISE

Hallelujah to The Great I am

Hallelujah to The Holy Lamb

Hallelujah to The King of Kings

Hallelujah to my God who's my Everything

Hallelujah to The Holy Infallible One

Hallelujah to Jesus my Savior, The Son of God

Hallelujah to Jehovah Shiloh my promised peace

Hallelujah to Jehovah Rapha my Healer, Redeemer and King

Hallelujah to The Lord of Host

Hallelujah to El Elyon, The God Most High for you're more than enough

Hallelujah to Jehovah Jireh, Hallelujah to my only source and Provider

Hallelujah to my Shield and Buckler

Hallelujah to my Protector for He is my Fortress and Portion

Hallelujah to Jehovah Nissi, The Lord my Banner who is always with me

Hallelujah to El, The Strong One

Hallelujah to Elohim, The Creator and all Powerful One

Hallelujah to El Shaddai, The All Sufficient One

Hallelujah to Jehovah, The Self-Existent One

Hallelujah to Jehovah Rohi, The Lord my Shepherd

Hallelujah to Jehovah Tsidkenu my Righteousness and Shelter

Hallelujah to El Elohe YIsrael, The God of Israel

Hallelujah to God with us Emmanuel

Hallelujah to Adonai my Great Lord

Hallelujah is the highest praise we can give to God forevermore

*O praise the Lord, all ye nations: praise him, all ye people. Psalms 117:1*

# Flo's Quotes

"If you claim to be Royalty…..you should think like it, speak like it, act like it, look like it and dress like it!

1 Peter 2:9 – "But ye are a chosen generation, a royal priesthood"

"I'm enraptured by the essence of your presence. Daily I honor you and give you reverence. God, I take pleasure in you, because you are my ultimate treasure. You gave your son Jesus, which can't be measured. These are my confessions!!!"

"God desires for us to assemble to worship with other believers of Christ. This will strengthen our faith, help us to run this kingdom race and it's all by grace."

"The Bible says your gift will make room for you. I believe before God present you to the world, He will first fine tune you."

"Don't reduce your standards being seduced by something that's counterfeit. Open your eyes and be introduced to something that's God sent."

"Don't become a prisoner of your own mind, by allowing artificial thoughts to dominate your paradigm. God sent His Word to give you a peace of mind, revelation and knowledge. After God gets finished with you, you will be spiritually polished. This will give you power to annihilate and abolish your former way of thinking."

"When you live a life of integrity.....God will honor you with His finest blessings."

"I use to look in the mirror and see my imperfections, while looking for other suggestions. I finally embrace what God thinks of me. He envisions His glorious reflection, despite another's rejection. Continually, I receive his never-ending love and affection."

"Satan is the author of confusion. I've come to the conclusion that God is the source of every solution. Learn to cancel all illusions."

"When you reach a certain stage and age in your life; some conversations shouldn't be entertained. God will give you wisdom."

"We should never estimate that God is late. Whenever He shows up, he's right on time and the feeling is quite divine."

"In life when you set expectations you don't reach, press the reset button. Restart the process. Begin to make progress because you're destined for great success."

"Children are full of life and laughter, but evil elements expose their innocence. We have the power through God to divert evil to good and the end result is victorious."

"Don't allow others to weaken your faith, because they don't have GREAT FAITH like you. Keep believing God to do BIG things in your life; it's your kingdom inheritance in Christ."

"God has already confirmed, finalized and approved; what can't be denied, rejected or disapproved."

"Women until you're identified and found by your husband….. make sure you're walking in purpose, fulfilling your destiny and wearing your royal crown."

"If you experience a loss, you don't have to lose your mind, identity, direction, purpose or vision. God will strengthen you through the healing process; for His strength is made perfect in weakness."

"It is you that complete me. Every fiber of my being is desperately chasing after thee. You have never lied to me and continue to love and embrace me unconditionally. This is your authentic love for me, which equates to infinity. God, I need you everyday and every hour. You are the only infallible one, who gives me strength and power. Without apprehension, I daily submit to you, so I can experience you at another dimension. I'm evoked to mention, when I feel alone, you give me your undivided attention. This is what calms and renews my spirit. It is you!"

"God will allow separation when you're in preparation for a major move and demonstration of the manifestation that he's about to perform in your life. Stay in expectation!"

"God sent His son Jesus to die for our sins. Receive him as your personal Lord and Savior. God will release to you His kingdom favor. Have faith and repent of your sins. Rom. 10:9 says, That if thou shalt confess with thy mouth the Lord Jesus, and shalt believe in thine heart that God hath raised him from the dead, thou shalt be saved. Every stain of your sins will be washed away, by the blood of Jesus. This is your new season!"

# Scripture References

- So then faith cometh by hearing, and hearing by the word of God. *Romans 10:17*

- Now faith is the substance of things hoped for, the evidence of things not seen. *Hebrews 11:1*

- But without faith it is impossible to please him: for he that cometh to God must believe that he is, and that he is a rewarder of them that diligently seek him. Hebrews 11:6

- For all have sinned and come short of the glory of God. *Romans 3:23*

- Therefore if any man be in Christ, he is a new creature: old things are passed away: behold, all things are become new. *2 Corinthians 5:17*

- For God so loved the world, that he gave his only begotten Son, that whosoever believeth in him should not perish, but have everlasting life. For God sent not his Son into the world to condemn the world; but that the world through him might be saved. *John 3:16-17*

- He that loveth not, knoweth not God; for God is love. 1 *John 4:8*

- For by grace are ye saved through faith; and that not of yourselves: it is the gift of God. Not of works, lest any man should boast. *Ephesians 2:8-9*

- That if thou shalt confess with thy mouth the Lord Jesus, and shalt believe in thine heart that God hath raised him from the dead, thou shalt be saved. *Romans 10:9*

- For he hath made him to be sin for us, who knew no sin; that we might be made the righteousness of God in him. 1 *John 4:4*

- Then Peter said unto them, Repent; and be baptized everyone of you in the name of Jesus Christ for the remission of sins, and ye shall receive the gift of the Holy Ghost. *Acts 2:38*

+ For God hath not given us the spirit of fear; but of power, and of love, and of a sound mind. *2 Timothy 1:7*

+ But ye shall receive power, after that the Holy Ghost is come upon you; and ye shall be witnesses unto me both in Jerusalem, and in all Judea, and in Samaria and unto the uttermost part of the earth. *Acts 1:8*

+ Behold, I give unto you power to tread on serpents and scorpions and over all the power of the enemy and nothing shall by any means hurt you. *Luke 10:19*

+ He shall give his angels charge over thee, to keep thee in all thy ways. *Psalms 91:11*

+ No weapon that is formed against you shall prosper and every tongue that shall rise against thee in judgment though shalt condemn, this is the heritage of the servants of the Lord and their righteousness is of me saith the Lord. *Isaiah 54:17*

+ The thief cometh not, but for to steal, and to kill, and to destroy: I am come that they might have life, and that they might have it more abundantly. *John 10:10*

+ Be sober, be vigilant; because your adversary the devil, as a roaring lion, walketh about, seeking whom he may devour. *1 Peter 5: 8*

+ Who his ownself bare our sins in his own body on the tree, that we, being dead to sins, should live unto righteousness: by whose stripes ye were healed. *1 Peter 2:24*

+ He sent his word and healed them, and delivered them from their destructions. *Psalms 107:20*

+ But he was wounded for our transgressions, he was bruised for our iniquities; the chastisement of our peace was upon him; and with his stripes we are healed. *Isaiah 53:5*

+ Therefore I say unto you, What things soever ye desire, when ye pray, believe that ye receive them, and ye shall have them. *Mark 11:24*

- Beloved, I wish above all things that thou mayest prosper and be in health, even as thy soul prospereth. *3 John 1:2*

- But thou shalt remember the Lord thy God: for it is he that giveth thee power to get wealth, that he may establish his covenant which he sware unto thy fathers, as it is this day. *Deuteronomy 8:18*

- Let them shout for joy, and be glad, that favour my righteous cause: yea, let them say continually, Let the Lord be magnified, which hath pleasure in the prosperity of his servant. *Psalms 35:27*

- Christ hath redeemed us from the curse of the law, being made a curse for us: for it is written, Cursed is everyone that hangeth on a tree: That the blessing of Abraham might come on the Gentiles through Jesus Christ; that we might receive the promise of the Spirit through faith. *Galatians 3:13-14*

- I will praise thee; for I am fearfully and wonderfully made: marvelous are thy works; and that my soul knoweth right well. *Psalms 139:14*

- And I will restore to you the years that the locust hath eaten, the cankerworm, and the caterpillar, and the palmerworm, my great army which I sent among you. And ye shall eat in plenty, and be satisfied, and praise the name of the Lord your God, that hath dealt wondrously with you: and my people shall never be ashamed. *Joel 2:25-26*

- For I know the thoughts that I think toward you, saith the Lord, thoughts of peace, and not of evil, to give you an expected end. *Jeremiah 29:11*

- For it is the day of the Lord's vengeance, and the year of recompenses for the controversy of Zion. *Isaiah 34:8*

- Dearly beloved, avenge not yourselves, but rather give place unto wrath: for it is written, Vengeance is mine; I will repay, saith the Lord. *Romans 12:19*

- But as it is written, Eye hath not seen, nor ear heard, neither have entered into the heart of man, the things which God hath prepared for them that love him. But God hath revealed them unto us by his Spirit: for the Spirit searcheth all things, yea, the deep things of God. 1 *Corinthians 2: 9-10*

+ There is therefore now no condemnation to them which are in Christ Jesus, who walk not after the flesh, but after the Spirit. *Romans 8:1*

+ So then they that are in the flesh cannot please God. *Romans 8:8*

+ But ye are a chosen generation, a royal priesthood, an holy nation, a peculiar people; that ye should shew forth the praises of him who hath called you out of darkness into his marvellous light: *1 Peter 2:9*

+ Now the works of the flesh are manifest, which are these; Adultery, fornication, uncleanness, lasciviousness, Idolatry, witchcraft, hatred, variance, emulations, wrath, strife, seditions, heresies, Envyings, murders, drunkenness, revellings, and such like: of the which I tell you before, as I have also told you in time past, that they which do such things shall not inherit the kingdom of God. *Galatians 5:19-21*

◆ But the fruit of the Spirit is love, joy, peace, longsuffering, gentleness, goodness, faith, Meekness, temperance: against such there is no law. *Galatians 5:22-23*

◆ I BESEECH you therefore, brethren, by the mercies of God, that ye present your bodies a living sacrifice, holy, acceptable unto God, which is your reasonable service. And be not conformed to this world: but be ye transformed by the renewing of your mind, that ye may prove what is that good, and acceptable, and perfect, will of God. *Romans 12:1-2*

◆ So shalt thou find favour and good understanding in the sight of God and man. Trust in the Lord with all thine heart; and lean not unto thine own understanding. In all thy ways acknowledge him, and he shall direct thy paths. *Proverbs 3:4-6*

◆ They that trust in the Lord shall be as mount Zion which cannot be removed, but abideth for ever. *Psalms 125:1*

- The angel of the Lord encampeth round about them that fear him, and delivereth them. *Psalms 34:7*

- Beloved, believe not every spirit, but try the spirits whether they are of God: because many false prophets are gone out into the world. *1 John 4:1*

- O praise the Lord, all ye nations: praise him, all ye people. *Psalms 117:1*

- All scripture is given by inspiration of God, and is profitable for doctrine, for reproof, for correction, for instruction in righteousness: *2 Timothy 3:16*

- Making the word of God of none effect through your tradition, which ye have delivered: and many such like things do ye. *Mark 7:13*

- Death and life are in the power of the tongue: and they that love it shall eat the fruit thereof. Proverbs 18:21

- Be not rash with thy mouth, and let not thine heart be hasty to utter any thing before God: For God is in heaven, and thou upon earth: therefore let thy words be few. *Ecclesiastes 5:2*

- So God created man in his own image, in the image of God created he him; male and female created he them. *Genesis 1:27*

- For to one is given by the Spirit the word of wisdom; to another the word of knowledge by the same spirit. *1 Corinthians 12:8*

- And God said, Let there be light: and there was light. *Genesis 1:3*

- Every good gift and every perfect gift is from above, and cometh down from the Father of lights, with whom is no variableness, neither shadow of turning. *James 1:17*

- And from the days of John the Baptist until now the kingdom of heaven suffereth violence, and the violent take it by force. *Matthew 11:12*

- For thou hast made him a little lower than the angels, and hast crowned him with glory and honour. *Psalms 8:5*

# References

The Holy Bible "King James Version"

*Webster Dictionary*, 1983

# Bio

I'm a native of Chicago, Illinois and I was raised on the Westside. I'm the youngest of thirteen siblings; I have seven sisters and six brothers. My parents were amazing; they were instrumental in my life and a great blessing to me. I graduated from Northwestern Business College and studied Business Administration at Roosevelt University. My love for writing developed sixteen years ago. I pray that my poetry build faith, bring healing, manifest deliverance, reveal revelation and encourage others.

CPSIA information can be obtained
at www.ICGtesting.com
Printed in the USA
BVHW070056170223
658686BV00003B/55